CELEBRATING FAMILY MILESTONES

CELEBRATING FAMILY MILESTONES

BY MAKING ART TOGETHER

DEBRA LINESCH

FIREFLY BOOKS

A FIREFLY BOOK

Published by Firefly Books Ltd. 2000

First Printing

Canadian Cataloguing in Publication Data	U.S. Cataloging-in-Publication Data
Linesch, Debra Greenspoon, 1953–	Linesch, Debra.
Celebrating family milestones: by making art together	Celebrating family milestones: by making art together / Debra Linesch. – 1st ed.
ISBN 1-55209-505-3	[104]p.: col.ill. ; cm.
1. Communication in the family. 2. Parent and child.	Summary: Family art projects that help families communicate and cope with change.
3. Life change events – Psychological aspects.	ISBN 1-55209-505-3
4. Art therapy. I. Title	1. Art Therapy. 2. Family Therapy. I. Title.
HQ755.85.L56 2000 646.7'8 C00-930881-4	615.85156 21 2000 CIP

Published in Canada in 2000 by
Firefly Books Ltd.
3680 Victoria Park Avenue
Willowdale, Ontario M2H 3K1

Published in the United States in 2000 by
Firefly Books (U.S.) Inc.
P.O. Box 1338, Ellicott Station
Buffalo, New York 14205

Design: Counterpunch/Linda Gustafson
Page Production: Linda Gustafson, Sue Meggs-Becker
Project Editor: Charis Cotter
Illustrator: Clive Dobson
Children's Artwork: Jonas Becker, Sebastian Becker, Zoe Cleland,
Jolie Dobson, Allison Worek, Katherine Worek

Printed and bound in Canada by Friesens, Altona, Manitoba

*The Publisher acknowledges the financial support of the
Government of Canada through the Book Publishing Industry
Development Program for its publishing activities.*

ACKNOWLEDGMENTS

There are many people who have contributed to the development of the ideas in this book. I want to thank all the children who did art projects in my classrooms throughout the City of Toronto between 1976 and 1979. I also want to thank all the children and families who did art projects in my therapy offices in a variety of clinical settings in the City of Los Angeles between 1980 and 1998. A special thank you to Natalie Spain, who understood the intention behind this book and contributed to its production with her creativity. And I want to thank my husband, my children and our neighbors and friends who did art projects in our homes, always.

WHY DO FAMILY ART?

In contemporary family life, where parents often work long hours and children have busy schedules of their own, it is more important than ever to find meaningful time to spend together. Making art together as a family provides a time and place for everyone to express themselves creatively as they experience the various changes, celebrations and milestones of family life. The creative process acts as a powerful force to help build a sense of family identity and cohesion, as well as giving each individual an opportunity to explore their unique role in the family structure.

Hopefully each project you do together will result in a lasting and treasured piece of family art, but the process is more important than the finished product. The communication, interaction and expression of feeling as you work provide a depth of experience that will enrich your family life.

No art project in this book is meant to be completely duplicated. The examples here are presented to demonstrate an attitude to making art and an approach to exploring family experiences. You can use your imagination to modify or expand the crafts to suit your family's particular needs.

The projects are not technically challenging. They have been chosen for their psychological value, requiring involvement, participation and enthusiasm rather than skill or artistic talent. Each craft will provide you with an opportunity to interact together, recognize important family events and enhance your collective sense of your family's identity.

The projects are divided into four sections.

Getting Started explores the process of developing the physical and psychological space for your family to get involved in art making. The other three sections are each based on a dimension of family life: Transitions, Passages and History.

Transitions illustrates creative ways to deal with experiences of loss and change: the birth of a new child, a grandparent's death, good friends moving away and a parent's business trip.

Passages explores ways to acknowledge and celebrate family passages. Birthdays, New Year's, Mother's Day and Father's Day are examples of times when making art can deepen your family's experience.

History suggests some ideas for incorporating your family's history into your present life. Family stories and photographs are used as resources to document your family's journey through time.

I hope this book will inspire you to get together as a family and make crafts that have meaning for you. Have fun!

CELEBRATING FAMILY MILESTONES

CONTENTS

INTRODUCTION

This book is the culmination of my work as an elementary school teacher, art psychotherapist and mother. Although many interesting and creative projects are presented within these pages, this book is not a "how-to" craft book. It has another purpose. All of the projects are designed to be done together with your family, bringing you closer through creative expression of the changes and milestones in family life.

This introduction contains the driving ideas that led me to write this book. The projects in the book will be much more useful to family life if the ideas behind them are clearly understood.

My ideas about children and art grew out of my experiences as an elementary school teacher. In the classroom I discovered the ways in which art projects supported learning and development. As a young teacher I was often frustrated with the rigidity of the curriculum for very small children, especially those who were struggling with cultural and language issues. As I began including more visual arts in the curriculum, I observed that children who had been grappling with the challenges of learning to read were able to support their faltering

The projects in the book will be much more useful to family life if the ideas behind them are clearly understood.

efforts at self-expression by drawing stories to illustrate their ideas. As their artwork clarified their meaning, their vocabulary and expressive efforts were augmented. Children who had limited confidence in their own ability to use language were able to build, construct and organize art projects. This prepared them to approach academic tasks with fresh enthusiasm and a renewed sense of mastery.

As I observed that children in my classes benefited in all aspects of classroom life from the inclusion of creative projects in their daily activities, I began to add more visual arts to my teaching strategies. Ultimately, convinced of the value of art in education, I left my career as a teacher to pursue a career in art psychotherapy.

My commitment to the visual arts remained central in my work as an art psychotherapist. For many years and in a variety of clinical situations I observed the ways in which individual and family development were supported by engaging in making art. I worked with young children who were able to use art to tell their horrific stories of abuse and abandonment for the first time. I worked with adolescent youngsters who were able to use art to articulate and support their struggles to create an identity and sense of self. I worked with families who were able to use art to identify and rectify destructive familial behavior. I witnessed countless examples of art making people's lives better.

Over time I became increasingly convinced that the visual arts could be as powerful in preventing problems and strengthening family life as the delivery of mental health services. I supported the inclusion of psychologically minded arts programs in community centers, public schools and public libraries.

Most importantly, however, my ideas about the role art-making can play in family life came to fruition when I had children of my own. Faced with the inevitable challenges and pressures of raising a family, I often turned to art-making as a parenting strategy. I came to motherhood convinced of the power of the visual arts in supporting emotional and familial growth. My experiences of parenting only enhanced that belief. My husband and two children have had a great influence on my decision to write this book.

Many people yearn to include creative endeavors in their family life and long for active participation in family rituals. Based on my observations and my experience of the richness of creating art with families, I offer you this book in the hope that it will encourage and inspire your family to make art together.

GETTING STARTED

A Family Endeavor

The art projects illustrated here are not complicated. You don't need special skills or supplies to make them. Their purpose is to allow your family to explore experiences and express feelings with an attitude of openness toward each other.

CREATING THE SPACE

It is important to give some thought to both the physical and the psychological space that the family art experience requires.

PHYSICAL SPACE

You can use the dining room table, the garage floor, the driveway or the coffee table. A room accessible to all family members is best, where people can join in easily and leave when they need to. A comfortable space in which you can make a mess is perfect.

PSYCHOLOGICAL SPACE

The art projects outlined in this book will be most meaningful if they are the result of full family collaboration.

Family art-making demands the full emotional participation of everyone in the family. Finding the time to do it together and having the supplies organized and accessible will give the projects the importance they deserve, and smooth the way for a positive collaborative experience. Enthusiasm and commitment, especially from the adults, are crucial to the success of these projects. As you begin to experiment with the process of making art, you will find that generational differences fall away. Adults, adolescents and children can each make their own contribution to the artwork. The art projects outlined in this book will be most meaningful if they are the result of full family collaboration.

TIME

Schedule a time for the project when everyone is available and has the energy to get involved. This will depend on your family's individual schedules, ages and needs. It should be a time when no one is under pressure to do something else. All the projects have been given an approximate time allowance: one to two hours is usually enough time to complete them, although some projects take place over a number of days or weeks.

ORGANIZATION

If your supplies are kept well organized and accessible you will find it much easier to start a project. They don't have to be expensive or high quality. You just need a good supply of materials in good condition. Knowing that your supplies are at hand will help generate the enthusiasm you all need to get going.

PREPARATION AND PLANNING

Before you start, check your supplies against the list of materials for the project. Make sure you have enough of everything to complete the project. When scheduling, allow time for glue or paint to dry. Some steps can be done first to make things easier, especially when working with very young children. Make sure the surface you are working on is protected by covering it with newspapers or dropsheets. If painting, have a supply of old shirts or aprons handy to cover up everyone's clothes.

PAINTING SHIRT

To make a lasting and very special cover-up, find an old shirt, preferably white. Buy some colorfast fabric paints that won't wash out. On a piece of paper, draw an outline of the shirt, front and back. Then work out a design with your child, sketching it on the paper where you can erase anything that doesn't work. You can divide the shirt into sections and sketch each section with a different design. Draw flowers growing up the sleeves, or animals, faces or a landscape. Plan the design upside down on the shirt, so that when the child is wearing it and looks down, the images will be right side up: for example, on this shirt the faces are smiling up at her. Once you're both happy with the design, your child can start to paint the shirt, one side at a time, following the paper pattern. Every time you start to do a messy family craft together, your child can wear the shirt. The shirt will be most effective if your child wears it backwards. Not only will it keep clothes clean, but the shirt will serve as a colorful reminder of where collective creativity can lead.

A JUMPING-OFF POINT

Think of the projects in this book as a jumping-off point for your family creativity. Hopefully the projects presented here will stimulate your family's imagination, and you will find many other ways to work together to create memorable family art experiences. Your family's interaction is the important factor. By doing some of these projects you will begin to develop an approach to art-making as a family.

Your family's interaction is the important factor.

FAMILY CRAFT BOX

The craft box illustrated on page 22 serves as an invitation to the family to enter into the experience of art-making together. You'll find several ways to adapt the craft box to your particular needs and available space, along with some other ideas for getting your family started on art projects.

FAMILY | CRAFT BOX

Time Frame
1 hour; ongoing

A craft box is useful for keeping art supplies and materials when storage space is limited. Making a family craft box is also a good way to begin the family art experience. The box itself can be thought of as the source for the family activity: opening it signals the beginning of a creative process and closing it marks the end. You can keep it closed and tucked away most of the time, and then bring it out on special art-making occasions. Opening the box and exploring its contents will become part of a cherished family ritual.

Your craft box will take on the character of your family as you decorate the outside with photos, drawings, pieces of fabric, beads or anything else your family finds attractive and useful. Everyone can participate in keeping the box filled with a variety of interesting materials: buttons, lace, fabric, ribbons, wrapping paper, greeting cards, paper, glitter, stickers and yarns. All family members can add materials to the box in between art-making sessions. This way your box will always be full and its contents will continue to surprise and delight everybody. The craft box can become a kind of family archeological dig, full of remnants of both shared and private experiences.

◆　◆　◆

Step 1: Choose a suitable box with a lid.

MATERIALS

- box with lid
- fabric
- glue
- glue gun (optional)
- paint
- photos
- kids' drawings
- magazine pictures

Boxes
- wooden box with lid
- cardboard box with lid
- cigar box
- chocolate box

◆ A cardboard box that is covered with coated paper (like a tissue box) can be transformed into a pretty box with spray paint. The coated paper makes an excellent smooth surface for the spray paint to adhere to. Be sure to spread newspapers under the box, and point spray well away from face.

Step 2: Decorate the outside of the box by whatever method your family prefers:

- Cover it with fabric, using glue to stick material to box. Rather than gluing the whole piece of fabric, apply glue only to the edge of the fabric that folds over the ends of the box.

- Paint pictures or designs directly on the box.

- Make a collage with family photos or kids' drawings and glue on box.

- Make a collage with pictures cut from magazines and glue on box.

See Family Craft Box Variations page 26 for more ideas for covering your craft box.

Step 3: Fill your box with art supplies: crayons, glue, scissors, tape, paper. Then add whatever you think will be useful: ribbons, old wrapping paper, buttons, foil, recycled greeting cards, lace, glitter and stickers. Let the whole family participate on an ongoing basis, collecting little things that can be used to make art and adding them to the craft box.

FAMILY CRAFT BOX VARIATIONS

Every family's craft box will be unique. By varying the shape, size, covering and decoration, you can create the box that suits your needs and reflects your family's character.

SHAPE

You can use a container that has some special significance for your family: an old trunk, basket, hatbox or suitcase. As long as it has a lid, or a lid can be easily made for it, any container will work.

SIZE

Size and space do not have to place limitations on your creation. A small container such as a wooden cigar box, a pencil box or a jewelry box can be decorated and used to hold special materials such as sequins, stars and stickers.

COVERING

Fabric: Old scraps of tablecloths, pillowcases and clothing may all be used to cover your box. Fabric that evokes memories and family connections is especially meaningful.

Burlap: Burlap is sturdy, wears well and is easy to sew other materials onto.

Canvas: Canvas is very durable, and paint goes on it easily.

Bamboo strips or twigs: These can be glued onto your box in various patterns to add an interesting texture.

Aluminum foil: For that shiny, glistening look, foil works well, but it is easily ripped.

Wallpaper samples: These can be glued onto your box as a collage.

Wrapping paper: Like aluminum foil, wrapping paper can be somewhat fragile, but you can make some interesting collages with it.

EMBELLISHMENT

Use glue, a glue gun or needle and thread to attach any number of decorations to the outside of your box: photos, pressed leaves (ironed between two sheets of waxed paper), buttons, beads, old toys, costume jewelry. The decorations can be as varied as your imagination allows.

OTHER
IDEAS

Making a family craft box is only one way to get your family involved in making art together. Here are a few more suggestions.

FAMILY ART CUPBOARD

An extra cupboard that can be used exclusively for storing your art supplies is ideal. Organize your materials inside and then decorate the outside of the cupboard. An easy way to do this is to nail a small bulletin board to the door and then use it to display photographs of your family art projects.

FAMILY SUPPLY EXCURSION

Take your family on a trip to your neighborhood secondhand or discount store. You can find all sorts of interesting (and inexpensive) materials to stimulate your creativity: fabric, boxes, baskets, decorations and interesting "junk." Add your new treasures to your craft box for use in future art projects.

FAMILY ART GALLERY

The kitchen fridge is a handy place to display children's art. Another quick way to showcase art is to string a clothesline across a room and then hang pictures from clothespins. You could also designate a whole wall or a corner of a room as your family art gallery. You can even have gallery openings and specially designed installations. A table with a glass top also serves very well as a space to display art, taped to the underside of the glass.

FAMILY PHOTO ARCHIVES

Taking a photo to record your family's artwork is a good way to show how much you value the experience. Put the picture in your family album; put it on a bulletin board or the fridge; use it for a holiday card; or make a special album just for photos of your art projects.

SECTION 2 | TRANSITIONS

Transitions challenge

the equilibrium of family life. Births and deaths cause major disruptions; temporary separations and changes bring their own level of upheaval. Whether the event is positive or negative, the balance of everyday life can be upset. The creative process acts as a powerful force to help the family integrate the transition. By working together to create art, members of the family can express their emotions and explore their shifting roles.

This section describes four art projects that address family transitions: a birth, a death, a parting from friends and a temporary separation from a parent. The approaches and techniques outlined in each project can easily be adapted to fit other experiences.

Birth Announcement
page 34

The birth announcement illustrates a way in which family members can express their experiences individually and then incorporate them to create a collective piece of art, much like a chorus of voices narrating a story.

Tribute to Grandpa
page 40
Building a family tribute for a loved one who has died involves a different approach. Here the family works together to build a structure, then they add meaningful objects to it individually. The tribute helps family members express their memories and their connections to the deceased.

**Neighbors' Book
page 46**

The book about neighbors moving away presents another approach to managing transitions. The idea here is to stimulate and document memory in order to create an emotionally significant souvenir. The technique of bookbinding was chosen because of the importance and permanence symbolized by a published book.

**Calendar for Mom's Trip
page 52**

The calendar for Mom's trip represents a fourth approach. The intention of this project is to ease the emotional experience of a separation between parent and child. The calendar provides a daily ritual that encourages communication and connection.

Variations are suggested for the projects to show how to adapt them to various family transitions. The Other Ideas section lists some different ways of marking transitions through art-making.

BIRTH

ANNOUNCEMENT

Nothing is more joyfully disruptive to family life than the birth of a new baby. In the excitement of the baby's arrival it can be difficult for everyone in the family to express and share their feelings about this strange and demanding new family member. Creating family art together gives everyone, especially the children, a chance to express themselves, connect with each other and create a new sense of family that includes the baby.

This art project shows how one family used art to help them through the transition. They created a timeline drawing that illustrated their experiences before, during and after the birth of the new baby. They cut out their individual efforts and glued them on a large piece of posterboard, so that everyone's experiences were displayed together as equally important.

The finished poster became a collection of the different voices in the family. Framing the poster adds a sense of completion and containment to the project, making the artwork and the feelings seem more important. This particular birth announcement represents the successful collaboration of a family that struggled to understand, articulate and manage a transitional experience.

◆　◆　◆

MATERIALS

- large piece of poster-board or foam board
- markers or crayons
- drawing paper
- scissors
- magazine pictures
- photos
- glue

Step 1: Take a large piece of posterboard and create a grid by dividing it into columns. You can draw in the lines to separate the sections, or use ribbons, the way this family did, to make 3-dimensional lines. If you want to draw a frame around the outside, do that now. Write the family names down the left side and the time periods across the top: "Before Baby," "Baby's Arrival" and "Our New Family."

Step 2: Give each member of the family a piece of drawing paper. Divide it into the same 3 time periods: "Before Baby," "Baby's Arrival" and "Our New Family." Everybody can illustrate each section by drawing pictures or making collages with cut-outs from magazines or family photos.

This is how Jake, 8, experienced the birth of his new little sister, Lily. His drawings show that he is aware of his shifting position within the family.

Step 3: Cut out the pictures and glue them on the poster.

Step 4: There are many different ways to frame your poster. Here are a few suggestions.

- Create a mat by gluing the poster on a slightly larger piece of colored posterboard.
- Draw a frame on the poster when you make your grid, and then color it in or decorate it with art supplies or found objects.
- Save the wrappings from the baby's presents, and cut them into different-sized sections. Piece together in a collage and glue onto the frame section.
- Glue pieces of wood, bamboo or ribbons around the edge of your poster.

Safety Tip
- When working with young children, some glue is bound to end up in their mouths, so use the non-toxic type. If you are using a stronger kind of glue, make sure the area you are working in is well ventilated.

Frame
- colored posterboard
- wood
- bamboo
- ribbon
- recycled gift wrap

Making a collective poster is a project that can be used to help families through a number of family transitions.

GRANDPARENT MOVING IN

When a grandparent moves into the family home, everyone experiences a sense of transition. A good way to quickly involve the grandparent in a family activity is to get everyone to help create a poster. The headings could be entitled: "Before Grandma Came to Live with Us," "Grandma Moves In" and "Our New Family."

MOVING TO A NEW NEIGHBORHOOD OR CITY

In any transition, something is lost, something is gained and something is experienced.

In any transition, something is lost, something is gained and something is experienced. To demonstrate this, the "Before" column could be filled with collages made from photos or drawings of the old house, to show what has been left behind. The "After" column could be made up of images of the new house and neighborhood. The center column, entitled "The Move," could be used as a place to express how each person experienced the day of the move. Some family members may want to draw pictures of the actual trip, recording scenery and distance, while others may choose to draw pictures which express how they felt.

GETTING MARRIED

When a single parent gets married, a new person joins the family. Like the project to welcome a grandparent, this is an opportunity to get the new family member involved, as well as giving other members a chance to acknowledge the change in the family structure. The same "Before," "During" and "After" kinds of headings can be used on the poster.

TRIBUTE | TO GRANDPA

Time Frame
2 hours

When a family member dies, creating an art project can help everyone deal with their grief. Children not only experience a keen sense of loss, they also often have trouble connecting with their grieving parents. A family project like this can draw the family together and give them an outlet for their grief and sadness.

Building a tribute to honor the memory of the loved one incorporates the healing qualities of creativity and ritual. You can build a simple wooden structure or transform an everyday container with decorations. Place inside it personal objects and photographs that evoke memories. This can be an ongoing process as items are added or removed over a number of days. Children especially will enjoy adding objects and arranging and rearranging them. Each member of the family can choose items that help them express their memories of the deceased person.

The tribute need have no particular religious significance. It represents the memory, mourning and transformation that a family experiences when a dear relative dies. Designing this tribute helps the family to express their grief, find comfort in being with each other and create a lasting legacy for everyone to cherish.

In this example, a family built a permanent wooden structure. Simpler versions can be made by finding a container already made. An orange crate was used in the model below.

◆   ◆   ◆

MATERIALS

- wood
- tape measure
- saw
- glue gun
- nails
- hammer

Personal Items
- photos
- medals
- jewelry

Natural materials
- stones
- crystals
- flowers

Step 1: Measure and cut wood to make a simple wooden box.

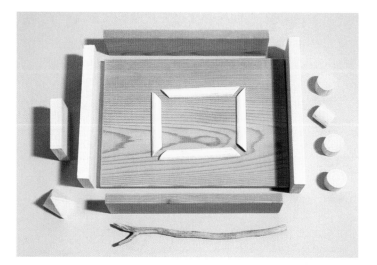

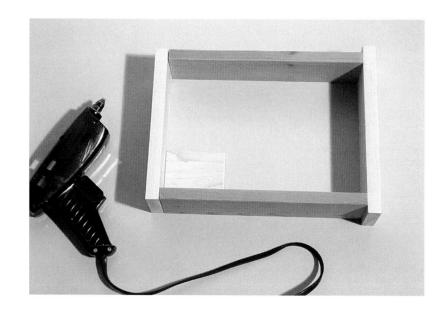

Step 2: Use either a glue gun or nails to attach the 4 sides to the back piece. You can make the base piece a little wider, as shown, to add stability.

Step 3: Cut a cylindrical piece of wood into 4 pieces to make the legs. Glue them to frame.

Step 4: To make an ornament for the top, make a little platform by gluing 4 wooden blocks to a larger square. Glue a triangular piece on this, topped by a wooden ball. Glue this whole structure on the top of the tribute.

Step 5: To make your own wooden frame for a photograph, take a piece of quarter-round molding and cut into 4 pieces, cutting diagonals at each end so they fit together. See photo, Step 1. Glue pieces together and use finishing nails to fit photo and cardboard backing to frame.

Step 6: Glue photo in middle of tribute frame. Choose personal items that evoke your relative's memory, like photos, jewelry, favorite books or treasured ornaments. Natural objects such as crystals, flowers, rocks or graceful branches can also help you to create a meaningful tribute.

If creating a tribute is not appropriate for your family, there are other projects you can do to help the grieving process.

MOURNING SCRAPBOOK

Buy a notebook or a scrapbook or make one by stapling or binding heavy paper together. Every day, write the date on a fresh page and leave it open for family members' contributions. They can draw pictures, write a few words, copy some lines of poetry, or glue in photos or something else that they associate with the deceased person. Periodically the family can gather and each person can have an opportunity to talk about what they have contributed to the scrapbook. As the experience of grief continues and evolves, the empty pages will gradually be filled up.

ROCK GARDEN

Making a rock garden is another way to acknowledge the grief and loss a family experiences when a loved one dies. This method is less direct than the altar and the scrapbook but it may suit your family better. The plants represent the possibilities for growth and renewal. Each member of the family should find a smooth stone, and then draw an image or write a word on it with indelible markers in memory of the deceased. Place the stones in a low shallow container and add water. Then plant small plants that will thrive in water. You can be inventive when choosing a container – a fish bowl, a glass flowerpot, a Pyrex casserole dish, a china serving dish – anything that will hold water and allow enough light for plants to root will work. A simpler variation of the rock garden is a memorial planter. If the deceased had a collection of houseplants, take cuttings from one or more of their favorite plants. Root in water, then plant together in a small planter or large flowerpot. The planter will become a living tribute to your loved one.

NEIGHBORS'
BOOK

Time Frame
2 to 3 hours, over a
period of a few days

When good friends move away, a joint project between the two families can help children express the depth of their friendships and the sadness they feel at parting. This particular book was created when two neighboring families were about to be separated. They decided to make a book together that they could keep as a permanent record of their friendship. The book was "published" in a limited edition of four copies, one for each child.

◆ ◆ ◆

Step 1: Help the children make up a simple story that describes the friendship and the move. Type or write one sentence per page on blank sheets of paper, leaving room for the children to draw pictures.

MATERIALS

- ◆ paper
- ◆ pencils, pens
- ◆ crayons, markers
- ◆ holepunch
- ◆ card stock
- ◆ string, ribbon or yarn
- ◆ scissors

Step 2: Distribute the pages to the children, letting them choose which line of text they want to illustrate. The kids can make a master drawing in color, to be color photocopied and distributed.

Sample Story

This is how the story unfolded for the Trans and the Rogers.

Page 1: The Tran family lived across from the Roger family for a long time.
Page 2: We did lots of fun things together.
Page 3: Hanna remembers the time when . . .
Page 4: Ethan remembers the time when . . .
Page 5: Tep remembers the time when . . .
Page 6: Mary remembers the time when . . .
Page 7: After many years of being neighbors the Trans moved away.
Page 8: Everybody feels a little bit sad.
Page 9: But we will still see each other.

Or they can make black and white line drawings, to be photocopied and then colored in.

Step 3: When all the drawings are finished, photocopy them so each child will have their own set of pages. If you have chosen to copy the pages in black and white, the children can color them in now.

Step 4: Each child can make a cover, using card stock or heavier paper. The books can be decorated with drawings or collages, and bound with ribbon or yarn from the family craft box.

NEIGHBORS' BOOK VARIATIONS

Writing, illustrating and binding books with children is a great way to get the whole family involved in an art project. The process is relatively simple and straightforward, and the end result is a permanent record of an important time in the family history. For example, the story of a summer vacation or special trip makes an interesting book, and you can glue in souvenirs gathered along the way, such as brochures, postcards, programs, ticket stubs or family photographs. You can add to the experience by experimenting with different methods of producing text, illustrations and binding, as well as adding publishing details.

Text: Use rhyming couplets instead of prose to tell the story. Younger children especially will enjoy the simple rhymes.

Illustration: Use photographs or torn paper collages instead of drawing.

Color: If you photocopy in black and white, you can use markers, paints, pastels or crayons to add color. Gold or silver metallic markers add a special touch.

Binding: The easiest way to bind books is to punch holes through the paper and covers and use rings or ribbons to tie them together. You can buy different kinds of binding products in office supply stores. For other examples of book binding, see Scrapbook Variations pages 80–83.

CALENDAR
FOR MOM'S TRIP

Time Frame
1 to 2 hours

A common source of anxiety for children and their parents is the prospect of a separation. A parent being away from home on a business trip, for example, can cause the child to worry about what will happen when the parent is away as well as to fear that the parent will never return. The primary goal of this art project is to contain these anxieties by creating a way for parents and children to connect, both before and during the separation. A calendar will break the time of separation into manageable periods and provide a reinforcement of the parent's love each day they are away.

Two calendars are made, with windows to open for each day of the trip: one for the parent, made by the child; and one for the child, made by the parent. A simple message is written underneath the flap. The windows can be opened by the parents and child at the same time each day, creating a ritual and an opportunity to connect to each other, even though parent and child are not in the same place. Children and grownups alike enjoy opening the little doors and finding the messages.

Completing this project allows both the parent and the child to anticipate the separation, measure the time apart and talk about any worries or concerns they might have.

The calendar can be adapted and simplified for very young children, or geared to older children who can write notes as well as draw pictures under the flaps. The first calendar shown here was made by a nine-year-old girl for her mother.

◆   ◆   ◆

MATERIALS

- posterboard or cardboard
- ruler
- pencils, crayons
- markers
- paint
- scissors
- glue

Optional Materials
- craft knife
- colored paper
- brass fasteners
- pipe cleaners
- ribbons
- stickers
- clear tape

Step 1: Cut 2 pieces of posterboard to the size you want for the finished calendar. Allow an area of about 4 x 4 inches for each day.

Step 2: Divide the first piece of posterboard into identical squares, one for each day you'll be separated. Draw boxes or other shapes in each square.

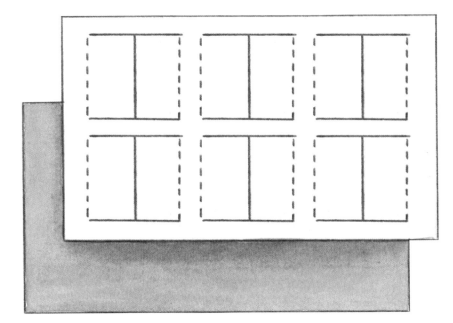

Cut on solid lines, fold on dotted lines.

Safety Tips

♦ Always supervise children when they're using knives. Teach them how to use them safely.

♦ Craft knives should be carefully put out of children's reach after use.

♦ The sharper the knife, the safer the knife. A dull blade won't cut cleanly and requires excessive force, which inhibits your control.

♦ Never cut on furniture. Use strong cardboard or wood underneath as a cutting surface.

Step 3: To create windows, cut out each shape as shown, leaving one side for the fold. Score the fold lines with a dry ballpoint pen, the back of a bread knife or a pair of scissors, and then fold to make a little double door that, when closed, covers the window and hides the message. If you like, use straight, wavy or diagonal lines to make each window different. See illustrations on page 56.

Step 4: After all windows are cut out and open, glue first piece of posterboard onto second piece by applying glue to the back of the first piece (i.e., the one with the cut-out doors). Do not apply glue to the backing cardboard, because that's where you are going to write the messages. Let dry and then give every window a date or number. Older children can relate to dates; younger children may just want to count the days before Mom returns.

Step 5: Repeat the process to make the second calendar, so that both the child and the parent will have a calendar to open during the separation. Vary the shapes of the doors to make each calendar different.

Scoring Tip

◆ When scoring paper or cardboard to make a good fold line, it is best to use something with a rounded edge, like a dry (used up) ballpoint pen or the back edge of a bread knife. The blade of a pair of scissors will work, but it tends to cut a little too sharply. To make the fold line really straight, score against a ruler.

Step 6: Now you and your child should each take your calendars and write messages or draw pictures in the windows and decorate the outside. To fasten windows, use tape, stickers, brass fasteners, ribbons or pipe cleaners.

Step 7: Give the calendars titles: "To Mom love Shannon," or "Mom's Trip to Chicago."

Step 8: Agree with your child that only one door will be opened each day at a jointly specified time. This gives her something to look forward to and the comforting knowledge that you are reading her message at the same time.

Finished Calendar

CALENDAR VARIATIONS

A variety of art projects based on the central theme of a calendar can be helpful whenever children need adult support to get through a difficult period: a separation from their parents, time spent in the hospital, or even the days leading up to a big event like a holiday or party. A calendar to mark time can be made in any number of ways. A few variations are shown below.

FLAPS

This example allows for greater creativity and a more interesting finished calendar. Older children and parents will enjoy making this, and little ones love opening and closing the flaps.

Step 1: Cut 2 pieces of cardboard to the same size. Corrugated cardboard is harder to cut than card stock (very stiff paper), which will work just as well.

Step 2: On a piece of paper draw different shapes, numbers and letters that you might like to use. Allow at least one straight side on each shape to fold for a hinge. Mark the hinge side with a red marker as a reminder of which side to score.

Step 3: Cut out shapes and arrange on first piece of cardboard. Trace with a pencil, marking the hinge side with a double line. Using a craft knife, cut out shapes, leaving hinge side attached. Score the hinges and fold back. Some of the shapes might not need hinges and can be cut out completely, like puzzle pieces.

Safety Tip

♦ When cutting paper and cardboard with a sharp knife, tape the work down to the cutting surface. Slowly rotate the cutting surface so you are always pulling the knife away from your hand.

Step 4: Glue or tape together the 2 pieces of cardboard. If using glue, apply glue only to the back of the piece from which shapes have been cut. Keep glue away from doors and the surface on which you are going to write. Write messages and decorate. You can also paint or use cut-out colored paper for different backgrounds under each flap.

Step 5: To make handles for the cut-outs, cut narrow strips of stiff paper, about 3 inches long and ½ inch wide. Fold in two and glue together. Make a score one third of the way along and fold, then glue to cut-outs.

ACCORDION CALENDAR

The accordion calendar is tactile and allows children to feel that they can hold time in their hands and manipulate its passage.

Step 1: Take a long piece of card stock and fold as shown. Using a ruler, score folds. Make as many folds as necessary to represent each day away. If the paper is not long enough, 2 pieces can be taped together. Be sure to make individual panels large enough to write or draw on.

Step 2: Write a message or draw a funny picture on the panel for each day.

Step 3: If you like, cut out stiff cardboard to make a durable front and back cover, and glue to the back of first and last pages. Decorate covers with photos, pictures from magazines, drawings, or whatever you fancy. To make a more permanent accordion book, see pages 81–83.

PUZZLE DRAWING

Here you will be making a simple jigsaw puzzle featuring art made by the parent and child. Each piece of the puzzle represents a day of separation.

Step 1: You will need 2 pieces of light card stock. To make the frame for your puzzle, take a standard piece of letter-sized paper (8 ½ x 11 inches) and carefully trace the shape of the paper into the center of one of the pieces of card stock. Be sure to leave at least 1 inch all around the outside of the area to be cut out. This will be the frame. Using a sharp knife, cut out the middle of the frame. Save the cut-out card stock to glue to the back of your picture later. Apply glue to the frame-shaped piece of card stock and glue it to the other piece, keeping the glue away from the edges.

Step 2: On the letter-sized paper, draw a picture that represents what you feel about each other, or how you are feeling about the trip. If you are making two puzzles, you can each draw a picture; otherwise draw it together. When finished, glue the picture to the piece of card stock you cut from the center of the frame.

Step 3: Turn the picture over and draw jigsaw-puzzle shapes on the back, one for each day of the separation. Number them. Using a very sharp craft knife, cut out the puzzle pieces.

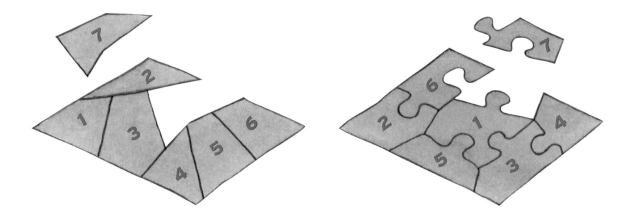

Step 4: Assemble the jigsaw puzzle inside the frame, making sure the pieces fit together.

Step 5: Decorate the frame with pictures or messages.

Step 6: Remove the puzzle pieces and place in an envelope. Each day the parent is away one piece is removed from the envelope and placed in the puzzle frame. The growing picture shows that the separation time is getting shorter.

CALENDAR FLIP BOOK

This is one of the easiest ways to make a calendar with your child.

Step 1: Take a pad of sturdy paper and assign one page for each day of the separation, removing any extra pages.

Step 2: Draw a set of cartoons, making slight changes on every page. Or write a message or draw a picture for each day.

Step 3: Your child can flip back and forth from day to day, noting the changes. Like the accordion, this calendar gives children the feeling that they can hold time in their hands.

OTHER | IDEAS

The birth announcement, the tribute to Grandpa, the book about the neighbors moving away and the calendar for Mom's business trip are all projects that help family members express and deal with the complex feelings that arise during transitions. You can invent art projects to ease many of the challenges your family encounters. The following ideas suggest creative ways to approach disruptive events.

SIBLING LEAVING FOR COLLEGE

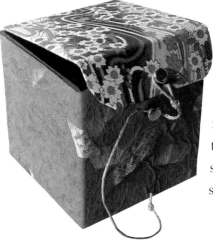

When grown children leave home to go to college, they often need to bring along some familiar icons of their childhood: an old doll, a favorite teddy bear or a treasured picture from their room. In their new and uncertain environment, they need to maintain a connection with home. The whole family can participate in making a small craft box for the student to take to college, filling it with special materials. The student can then make cards or pictures to send home or to friends left behind.

ILLNESS OF FAMILY MEMBER

Make get-well cards using a
simple pop-up design.

CHILDREN CHANGING SCHOOLS

Make diplomas to mark the
change from one school to
the other. The diploma will
represent a formal recogni-
tion of the end of one experience and the beginning of
another.

PASSAGES

In contemporary family

life, where parents often work long hours and children have busy schedules, it can be difficult to find time to celebrate passages. Special days and events offer a rich opportunity for families to make art together, providing an alternative to more commercial types of celebrations. The three projects described here involve everyone in a process that includes thoughtful communication and support for individual identity within the family.

Birthday Canisters
page 70

Making Birthday Canisters is a unique way to celebrate birthdays. The process helps family members to recognize that everyone has a contribution to make. This wonderful project has an extended life: the canisters can be used birthday after birthday in a significant family ritual.

Mother's Day and Father's Day Figures
page 72

This project gives children an opportunity to celebrate Mother's Day and Father's Day by creating figures of their parents. With only a little help, they can use their imaginations and the materials in the family craft box to create colorful and meaningful gifts for their parents.

**New Year's Scrapbook
page 76**

The New Year's Scrapbook
provides a simple way to
review the past year and
anticipate the year ahead.
The family can use this art-
making experience to
express their hopes, fears,
accomplishments and
disappointments.

Each of these projects illustrates a specific
life passage or holiday: birthdays, Mother's Day,
Father's Day and New Year's. You can use the same
process of exploration and discovery to celebrate
other milestones. See Other Ideas at the end of
this section.

BIRTHDAY
| CANISTERS

Time Frame
1 hour

Birthdays provide families with the opportunity to celebrate each family member's special day. Art-making can develop into a ritual that helps to emphasize the importance of each member of the family. Birthday canisters are fun and easy to make and can be used over and over again.

Everybody decorates their own canister in whatever style they wish. The finished containers will reflect the personality of the creator. A week before the birthday, the canister is set out in a prominent place and everyone is encouraged to write little messages or draw pictures and place them in the canister. On the birthday you can make a ritual of opening the canister and reading the messages. The messages can be kept from year to year, to be enjoyed and added to as time goes by.

◆　◆　◆

Step 1: Find an empty container with a lid.

Step 2: Decorate it by gluing on paper, fabric, or found objects. You can also use paint, or try wrapping it with ribbons, string or rubber bands for an interesting texture.

Step 3: Every birthday, give the family a week to add messages to the canister. Open it on the birthday and read the messages aloud. Keep the messages year to year in separate envelopes, to build up a collection of birthday wishes.

MATERIALS

- glue
- paint

Recycled containers
- coffee cans
- large yogurt containers
- ice cream cartons
- cardboard boxes
- hatboxes
- tins

Decorating materials
- *Paper:* tissue paper, wrapping paper, foil, construction paper, wallpaper
- *Fabric:* denim, cotton, felt, scraps of old clothing
- *Organic materials:* leaves, twigs, acorns, nuts, seeds, pressed flowers, feathers
- *Found objects:* ribbons, braiding, lace, cotton balls, beads, string, rubber bands, sequins

MOTHER'S
DAY AND
FATHER'S DAY FIGURES

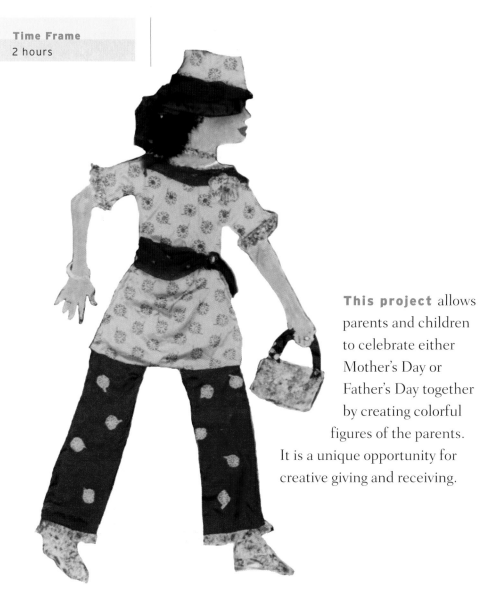

Time Frame
2 hours

This project allows parents and children to celebrate either Mother's Day or Father's Day together by creating colorful figures of the parents. It is a unique opportunity for creative giving and receiving.

This project accomplishes two goals: the family works together to create a special piece of art, and the children are given the opportunity to create symbolic tributes to their parents. The pictures can be made either life-size or in miniature, depending on your time, space and resources.

◆   ◆   ◆

Step 1: To make a life-size portrait, have the subject (either Mom or Dad) lie down on a very large piece of paper. The child can arrange the parent in a favorite pose. Then the child can take a pencil and trace the outline of the parent. In our example the mother was traced as if she was walking, and the father was traced as if he was waving to someone. No tickling!

MATERIALS

- large sheet of sturdy paper
- pencils
- scissors
- glue
- foam board
- old clothing
- fabric
- colored paper
- colored tissue paper
- crayons
- paints
- costume jewelry

Step 2: If you want to mount your picture on something permanent, glue it to a large piece of foam board.

Step 3: Cut out the silhouettes of the figures.

Step 4: Now the child can "dress" Mom or Dad. Using old clothes, fabric, colored paper, tissue paper, or just crayons or paints, the child can create clothes and accessories. This is a chance to use imagination, dip into the family craft box or the dress-up box, and have fun. Costume jewelry, old scarves or ties can be glued onto the figure.

If you decide to make a smaller portrait, the child can just draw a picture of the parent on a piece of sturdy paper, then glue it to foam board or cardboard, cut it out, and decorate it. Or photocopy a photograph of the parent, glue the photocopy onto foam board, cut it out and decorate.

Time Frame
1 to 2 hours, once a year

Family scrapbooks offer a rich opportunity for reflection. By using the scrapbook to look back on the year just passed, as well as to look forward to the coming year, you can develop an end-of-the-year ritual that will serve as an evaluation and an expression of anticipation for everyone in your family. Over the years the scrapbook will become a valued document of family life, marking changes, accomplishments and disappointments. It will be interesting to watch how your scrapbook evolves year after year as you address the important questions that define family life.

MATERIALS

- scrapbook
- markers, pens
- photos
- old magazines
- glue

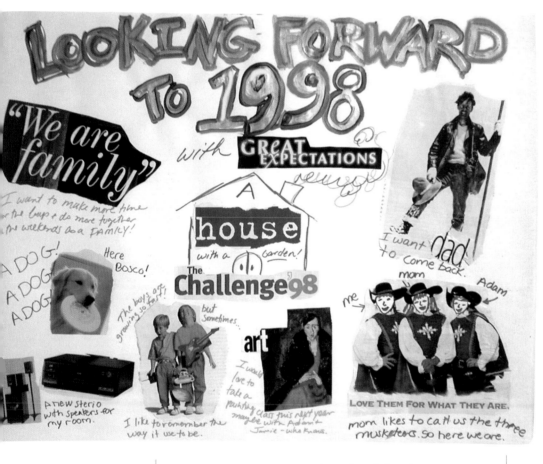

The scrapbook will be like a family's Christmas letter to themselves: a quick history of the high points of their year, as well as an outline of their plans for the next.

◆　◆　◆

Step 1: Buy a simple scrapbook at a stationery store. On two facing pages write the titles "Looking Back on [year just passed]" and "Looking Forward to [year to come]."

Step 2: Now the family can fill in each page with images and words that reflect their experiences in the past year and their hopes for the year to come. Use family photos, pictures cut from magazines or drawings. Even the youngest child can make a contribution of a simple picture or a wish dictated to an older child or an adult.

Step 3: Create a cover for the scrapbook with fabric, beads, drawings or materials found in your family craft box.

Step 4: Every year, repeat the process, looking back to earlier years for reference points.

SCRAPBOOK VARIATIONS

INDIVIDUAL SCRAPBOOKS

For growing families, especially those with teenagers, the large family scrapbook may not work. Individual scrapbooks give children more opportunity for independence. Each child may want to create their own scrapbook, where they can go into more details about their lives, as well as including family events.

HOMEMADE PAPER

Making your own paper can add a meaningful dimension to the process of creating a family scrapbook. If you make it using recycled materials, even better! Throughout the year, save paper such as greeting cards, event programs or special pages of schoolwork, and use them to make the pages to be bound into a scrapbook. Punch holes in the paper and use the blank side to write or draw on. Bind the pages together with ribbons, raffia or string. This is an excellent way to remember important events and incorporate them into your family memories.

ACCORDION BOOK

You may choose to make your own book, rather than buying one. An accordion book is easy to make with supplies you have around the house.

◆   ◆   ◆

Step 1: Take a long piece of blank paper and fold accordion-style, as shown.

Step 2: To make the front and back covers, cut 2 pieces of stiff cardboard just slightly bigger than a page of your accordion.

Step 3: Measure and cut 2 pieces of fabric or fancy paper ½ inch larger than cardboard. Cut off corners on the diagonal. Apply glue to edges of fabric and fold the fabric over cardboard.

Step 4: Apply glue to edges of the end papers of accordion and stick paper to inside of covers.

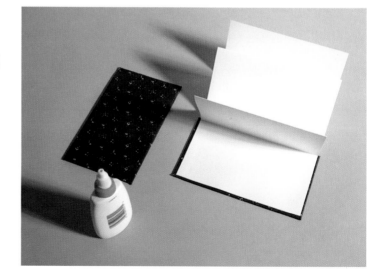

Step 5: Now the book can be filled in with a story, pictures, poems or collages. You can use this book for an individual scrapbook, a diary, a calendar for when a parent goes away, a special birthday card or a story written for a grandparent. Even very young children can get involved with making a simple book like this, and they will certainly enjoy drawing pictures on the pages.

OTHER | IDEAS

The projects described above help families deepen their experiences of passages in life. An art-making experience can be used to honor any special event that brings families together. The following ideas suggest different ways to use art to celebrate these times.

VALENTINE'S DAY HEARTS

Cut out two identical hearts for each member of your family from red felt or some other sturdy fabric. Using fabric-marking pens or embroidery, each person writes their name on a heart. Then give everyone a chance to write a message, draw a picture or add decorations to everyone else's heart. Sew each pair of hearts together and stuff with cotton. On Valentine's Day, make a special presentation of each heart to its owner.

THANKSGIVING BASKET

This holiday can be celebrated by decorating baskets that represent both thankfulness and hope for the future. Cut out pictures from magazines or draw pictures of things for which family members are grateful. Use these images to make a collage on the inside of a small wicker basket. On the outside, make another collage using images of things the family hopes will happen in the future. To make the decorations permanent, cover the basket with Mod Podge® or white glue diluted with water.

THANKSGIVING LEAVES

Collect some attractively colored leaves and press them between two sheets of wax paper, using a warm iron. The wax will transfer to the leaves and preserve them. Each member of the family can write something they are thankful for on a small piece of paper, and then glue the paper to the back of a pressed leaf. Use the leaves as decorations for your Thanksgiving dinner table. You can place one on each person's plate and then take turns reading out the messages.

One of the pleasures of being a parent is sharing stories and images of family history with your children. They may ask, "tell me a story of when you were little," or "who was my great-great-great-great-grandmother?" or "was Granddad a pioneer?" As they forge their own identities within their immediate families, children need to have a sense of where they come from and who came before them. Photo albums, videos and scrapbooks offer children glimpses into their family history that can enrich their developing sense of themselves. Interactive art projects can enhance the experience of sharing family history.

The Genogram Scroll, the Family Staircase and the Family Tree demonstrate how making art together can deepen a family's experience of their history, by documenting and then incorporating the past into the family's present.

**The Genogram Scroll
page 90**

The Genogram Scroll is a different type of family tree. Family members are depicted as colorful three-dimensional figures that are connected with ribbon to show their ties.

**Family Staircase
page 96**

The Family Staircase illustrates the associations between family members and previous generations.

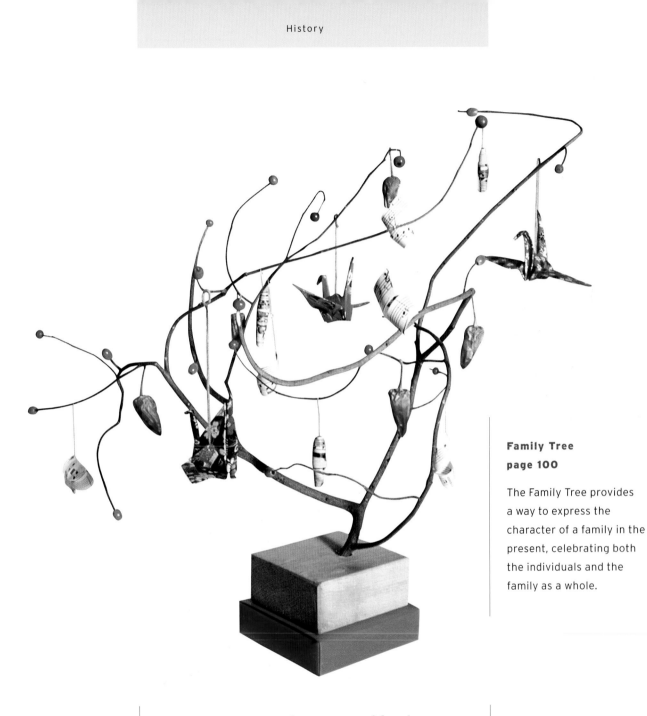

**Family Tree
page 100**

The Family Tree provides
a way to express the
character of a family in the
present, celebrating both
the individuals and the
family as a whole.

For more ideas on how to record family
histories, see Other Ideas at the end of this section.

GENOGRAM
SCROLL

Time Frame
2 to 3 hours

Children love making family trees and hearing stories about family members: aunts, uncles, cousins, grandparents, great-grandparents. Making a genogram scroll together will give you and your children an opportunity to explore your family history and clarify the relationships between the different generations. You may need to do some research: making phone calls and writing letters to relatives, digging out old photographs, asking grandparents about distant cousins. Your family's history will gradually be revealed, like the solution to a detective story, giving everyone the satisfaction of discovery and involvement.

The genogram scroll shown here was a labor of love: each family member was carefully drawn and then their clothes were made with colored tissue paper. To show their connections, the figures were linked by bits of ribbon from the family craft box.

◆   ◆   ◆

Step 1: Take a large roll of brown wrapping paper and stretch it out so you can start in the middle. Draw your immediate family members.

Step 2: Tear up bits of colored tissue paper and glue to the figures to make their clothes.

MATERIALS

- roll of brown wrapping paper
- pencils
- crayons
- markers
- colored tissue paper
- glue
- ribbon or yarn
- wooden sticks or bamboo poles
- fabric for cover
- silk rope

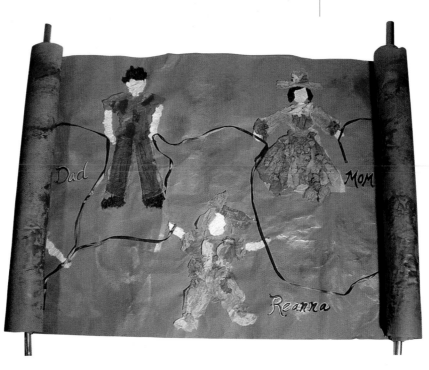

Step 3: Glue ribbon or yarn to the paper to connect the family members to each other.

Step 4: Start filling in the paternal family on one side of the scroll and the maternal connections on the other. Illustrate their style of clothes according to their characters and time period. Use old photographs if they're available to give you an idea of what clothes they wore. Again, use ribbons or yarn to connect each figure to the others.

Step 5: When your scroll is complete, glue ends to sticks or bamboo poles so you can roll it up.

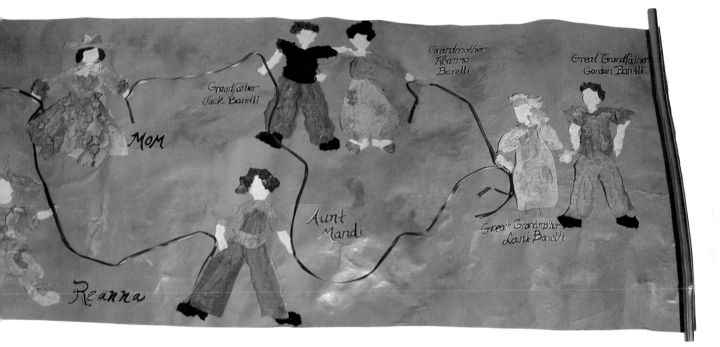

Grandfather
Jack Barelli

MOM

Grandmother
Reanna
Barelli

Great Grandfather
Gordan Barelli

Aunt
Mandi

Great Grandmother
Lanie Barelli

Reanna

Step 6: Sew a cover for your scroll from a richly textured piece of fabric. Use a silk rope to bind it.

GENOGRAM VARIATIONS

The important point about making a genogram scroll is exploring family history with your children. The goal is to connect with each other. You don't have to spend hours making an elegant work of art. Try some of these variations, or create your own version of the scroll.

- Use a smaller roll of paper, or a large piece of posterboard.
- Use markers or paint to portray the family members.
- Use fabric or colored construction paper to form the figures.
- Draw the connecting lines between the figures, rather than gluing on string or ribbon.

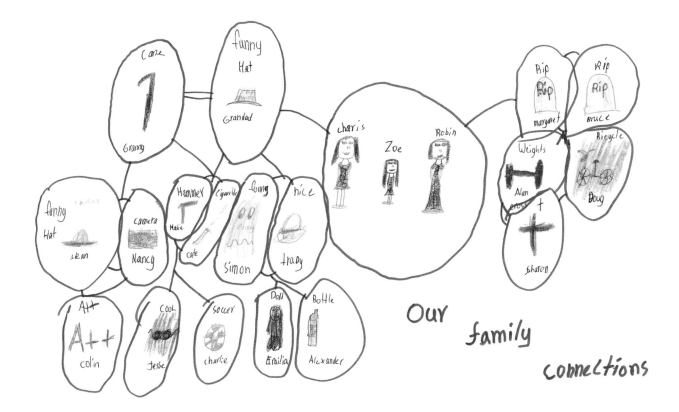

Our family connections

GENOGRAM POSTER

Children will often surprise you with their creative variations on a family craft in progress. Here the child got bored with drawing figures and asked if she could use symbols to represent the other people in her family. Everyone had fun choosing the perfect symbol for each person. The child took great satisfaction in drawing graves for her dead grandparents, sunglasses for her cool older cousin, a funny face for her uncle who was a comic, and funny hats for both her grandfather and her uncle, who shared a preference for strange headgear. The result was an amusing thumbnail sketch of her family, created with affection and humor.

FAMILY
| STAIRCASE

Time Frame
2 hours

This project was undertaken by a single-parent family after an elderly grandmother came to live with them. The father, children and grandmother created a family sculpture to celebrate

Christmas together. However, you can make a family staircase without relating it to any particular holiday. The different levels or stairs can represent different generations, phases or elements of family life.

In this example, the grandmother offered her memories of past holidays, the father was able to appreciate his role as the connection between the two generations before and after him, and the children broadened their family perspective on the holiday season. They used storytelling and creativity to collaborate on this memorable family art.

A simple staircase structure was created from Styrofoam, with different levels to represent each generation. Old photographs were photocopied and then cut out, glued to Styrofoam backing and mounted on the steps. Symbolic objects were chosen to represent important elements of family life. Some dollhouse furniture was found that had particular significance for the various members of the family. The grandmother chose the piano to illustrate the importance of music in her early life, something the children were not aware of before this project began. The father chose a clock to show his awareness of and sadness about the passage of time. The children chose an elegant, old-fashioned chair – perhaps to represent their grandmother, who had so recently moved into their family home. They embellished their sculpture with Christmas tinsel.

◆   ◆   ◆

MATERIALS

- photos
- scissors
- foam board
- white glue
- Styrofoam
- long nails
- colored tissue paper

Decorations
- found objects
- Christmas tree decorations
- dollhouse furniture
- fabric
- ribbons

Step 1: Ask each generation of your family to collect family photographs.

Step 2: Choose one special photograph from each generation.

Step 3: Photocopy the pictures, enlarging them if necessary. Cut out silhouettes of the figures.

Step 4: Trace the silhouettes onto foam board and cut to make backing. Glue silhouettes onto foam board to create standing forms.

Step 5: Using Styrofoam, build a staircase of three (or more) levels to represent the generations involved in the project. You can use glue to stick the stairs together, or, as in this example, long nails. These were used later to mount the standing forms. For a more realistic-looking staircase, make a banister with Popsicle sticks or twigs and glue to the Styrofoam.

Step 6: Tear different colors of tissue paper in long strips. Mix white glue with a little water in a bowl. Dip dampened tissue paper in this mixture and then wrap the tissue around the nails. Next, layer the tissue carefully over the Styrofoam, overlapping until all the surface is covered. The dye from the tissue paper will bleed and run when soaked in glue, creating a pretty, mottled effect. When the glue dries, your structure will have an attractive, glossy finish.

Step 7: Glue the standing forms to the tall nails.

Step 8: Now ask each member of the family to talk about their memories, either of celebrations of holidays or just day-to-day life together. This part of the project is just as important as actually making the craft. Hopefully you will discover things about each other that you didn't know before. From your discussion of the past and the present, choose objects to add to the staircase. Here's where you can have fun with your imagination. If somebody liked to dance, for example, you can find a way to represent that, perhaps with a little ballerina doll. Or if the family loved to play Scrabble, you can collect some old Scrabble letters. Get everyone involved in deciding what objects to add to your staircase.

Step 9: Glue the symbolic objects on the appropriate level. In this model, the first step represents the children and the present, the second the father and his past, and the third the grandmother and her family.

Step 10: If you wish, decorate your staircase. Dig into your family craft box and use ribbons, tinsel or scraps of fabric to embellish your creation.

FAMILY | TREE

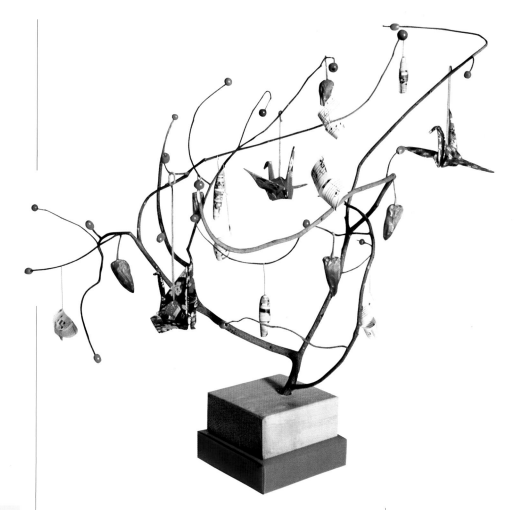

Time Frame
2 hours

Some families may not want to focus on family history, but to celebrate instead their current family configuration. A good way to do this is to make a literal family tree, using a branch with as many shoots as there are family members. Each family member can decorate their shoot according to their character and interests. The resulting sculpture will illustrate each member's individuality while emphasizing their family connections.

◆ ◆ ◆

Step 1: Find a tree branch that can be trimmed so that each family member has their own shoot.

Step 2: Each person can wrap their shoot with a different color of twine.

Step 3: Create personal ornaments to hang from the shoots. Each person can express their interests and character by the ornaments they make. A musician made these little paper scrolls with musical notes drawn on them. A person who loved origami made birds. Use your imagination. A great reader might make little paper books, a runner might hang doll's running shoes and someone who loves to cook could hang a tiny saucepan.

MATERIALS

- Tree branch

Materials to cover branches
- colored twine
- velvet
- fabric
- tissue paper
- raffia
- ribbons

Ornaments to hang
- beads
- shells
- stones
- crystals
- tissue-paper flowers
- tiny dolls
- dollhouse furnishings
- feathers
- tiny toys
- origami

FAMILY TREE VARIATION

Young children will especially enjoy making this easy family tree. The branches and leaves are made from cut-outs traced around family members' hands. Use just the immediate family, or for a really big tree include grandparents, aunts, uncles and cousins. This project creates a visual expression of the family as one entity made up of individuals.

◆ ◆ ◆

Step 1: Using different colored construction paper (green for a summer tree, or different shades of yellow, orange or red for a fall tree), trace all the hands of your family members, writing names with markers or crayons. Cut out the paper hands.

Step 2: Cut the trunk from green or black construction paper.

Step 3: Glue trunk to large piece of paper; arrange the hands as the branches; then glue.

OTHER
IDEAS

Just as the Genogram, the Family Staircase and the Family Sculpture help families incorporate a sense of their own history, other kinds of art projects can help families gain and articulate a sense of their relationship to the past. Here are two different ways to help reinforce your appreciation for family history.

FAMILY QUILTS

Cut out felt squares in several colors and mail them to all family members, asking them to draw, embroider or appliqué their names and dates of birth. When the patches of felt are returned, glue or sew them to a larger piece of fabric to create a colorful record of family history. You can make this as extensive as you want to. If you want to include more names, ask your relatives to make squares for their parents and perhaps their grandparents, tracing your family as far back as you can. If some family members are unwilling to participate in actually making the squares, ask them to provide you with the information. Your family can make quilting squares for them.

JOURNEY MAPPINGS

Take a large map of the world and show where your family came from, using ribbons and pins or tape. Use different colored ribbons for different branches of the family. For example, if your side of the family moved from Poland to New York, stretch a blue ribbon from one country to the other, attaching it to the city at either end with a push pin or tape. If your spouse's family moved from Jamaica to Toronto to San Francisco, string a red ribbon between each country and destination. The finished map will provide a visual reference of your family's origins. If your family has always lived in the same city, make a travel map of all the places family members have visited. The scope of your map will depend on how extensive your family's travels have been.